At the
Hospital

Grateful Acknowledgement is made to
Bill Kottmann
Joan Wedge
Edward Health Services Corporation
Naperville, Illinois

Design and Art Direction
Lindaanne Donohoe Design

Illustrations
Penny Dann

Picture Acknowledgement

Courtesy of Edward Health Services Corporation — Cover, 3, 4,
6, 8, 10, 12 14, 16, 18, 22, 24, 26, 28 30

©Phil Martin — 20

• • • • • • • • • • • • • • • • • •

Library of Congress Cataloging-in-Publication Data

Moses, Amy.

At the hospital/by Amy Moses.
p.   cm.
Summary: Simple text and photographs present a hospital,
its people, and its objects.
ISBN 1-56766-291-9 (smythe-sewn library reinforced: alk. paper)
1. Hospitals — Juvenile literature. 2. Hospital care — Juvenile literature.
[1. Hospital. 2. Hospital care.] I. Title.

RA963.5.M665   1998   97-6933
362.1'1—dc21   CIP
                                                            AC

At the
Hospital

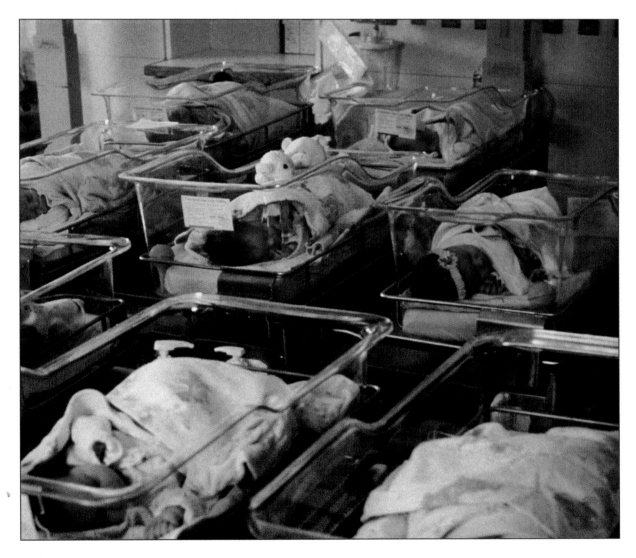

By Amy Moses

The Child's World

A hospital is a very busy place.

Nurses and doctors work there day and night.

They make sure every patient is cared for.

If a patient needs some help, they ring a bell and someone comes.

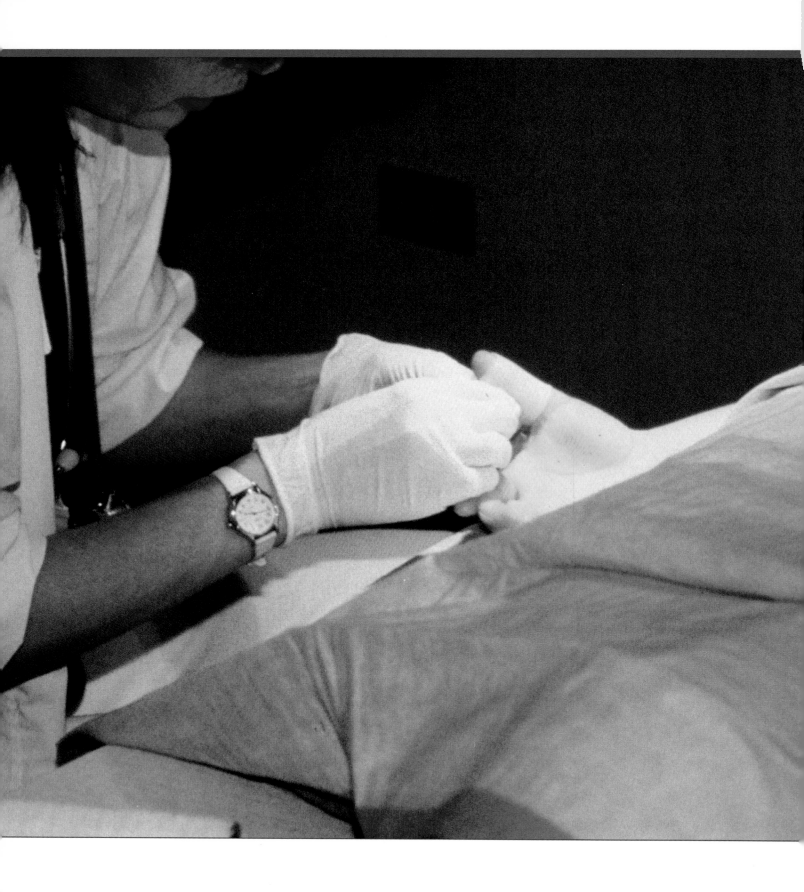

If someone needs stitches or breaks a bone,
they go to the Emergency Room for help.
A doctor may sew up a bad cut.
X rays are taken of a broken bone.
Then the bone is set and put in a cast.

Emergency Rooms are open twenty-four hours a day.

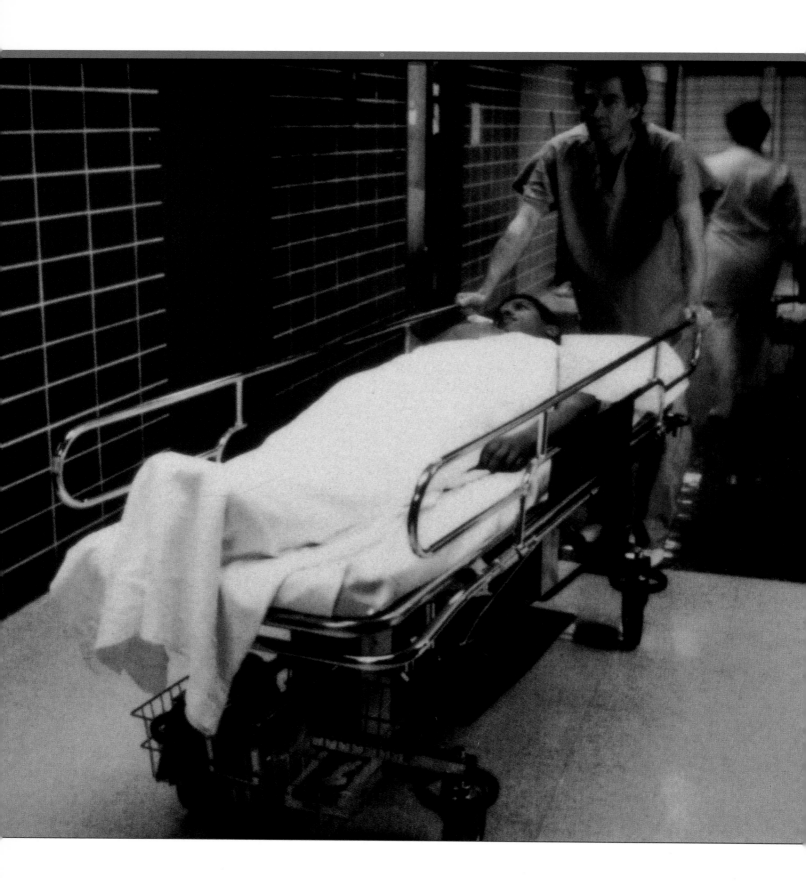

Sometimes a sick person has to go to the hospital. The patient checks in at Admissions and is given a room. An orderly takes the patient up to his or her room.

Orderlies move patients on gurneys and in wheelchairs.

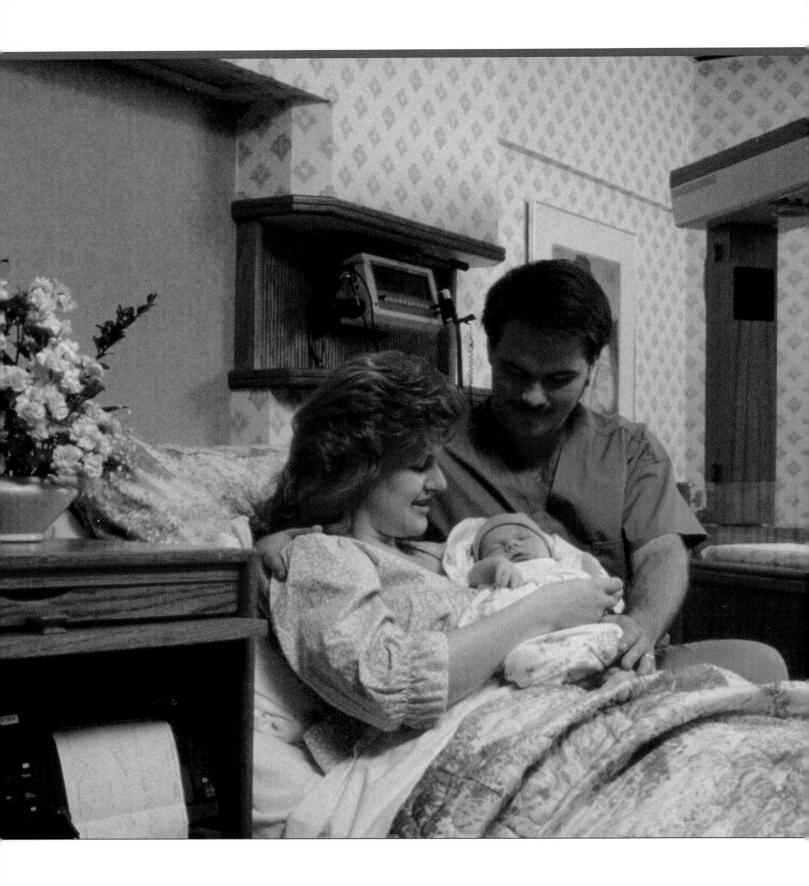

The people who run the hospital try to make the rooms cheery. They want the patients to feel at home. If the patient wants to call for help, they push a button. Another button will make the bed move up or down.

It is not a good idea to raise the top and bottom of the bed at the same time.

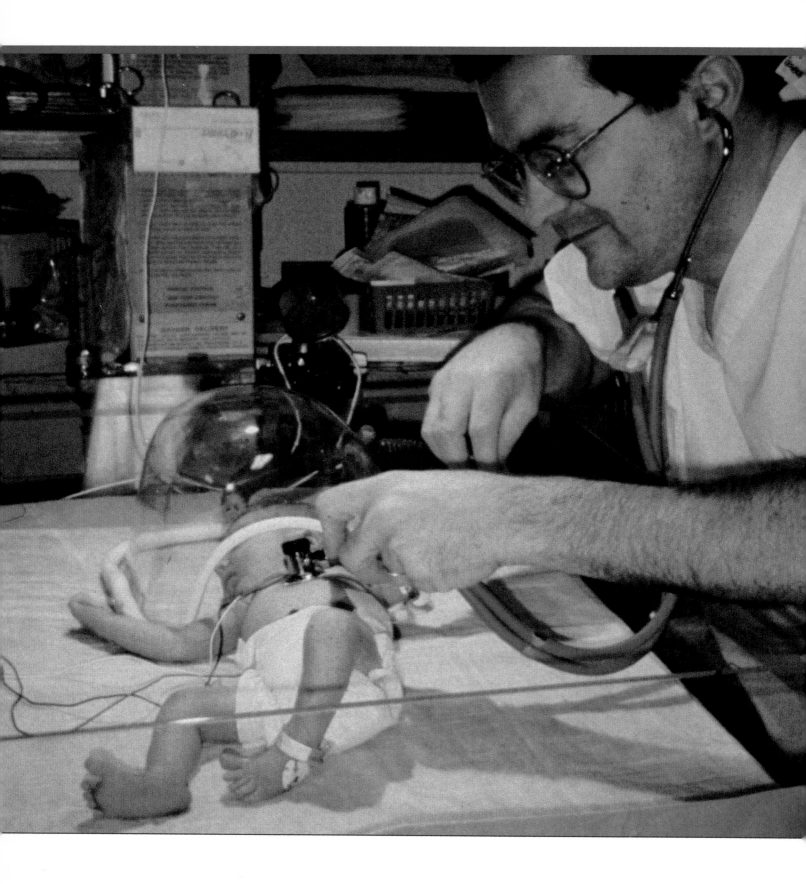

Some patients are very young.

Babies who are born too early are called "preemies."

They need special care.

Preemies need oxygen to help them breathe.

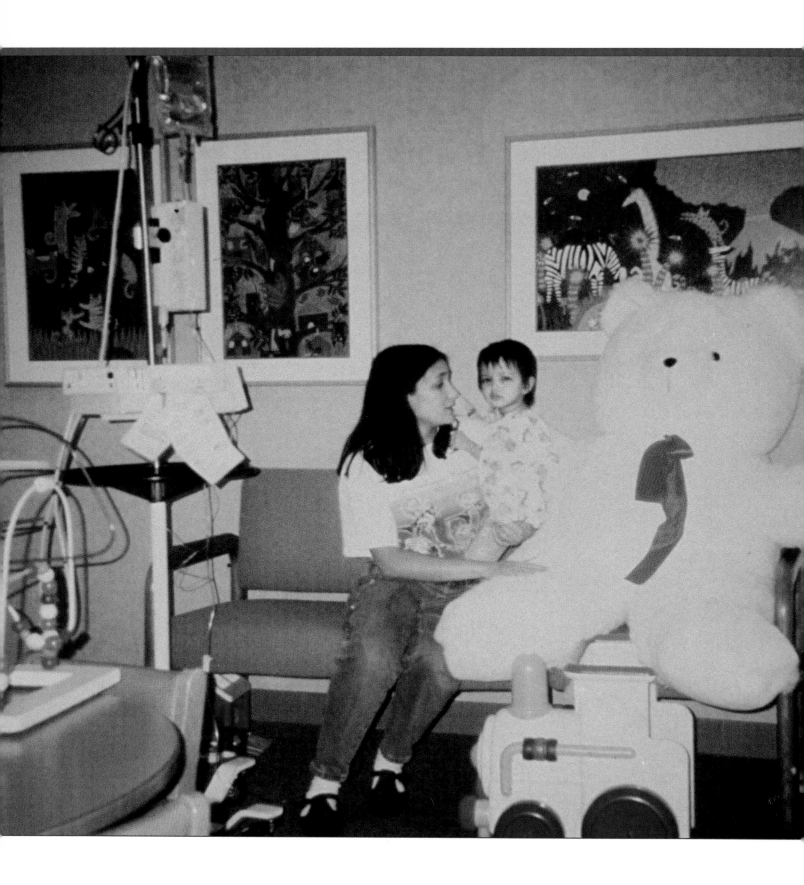

Hospitals have special rooms and special toys for children.

Children's wards are decorated in bright colors.

Some children have to stay in the hospital for a long time. Hospitals have teachers for these children so they can keep up with their schoolwork.

Entertainers come to perform for the children.

Hospitals let mothers and fathers stay with their sick children.

Children can make new friends in the hospital.

Dietitians make sure everyone gets healthy meals.
A hospital kitchen is a busy place.
Many meals have to be cooked and served
at the same time.

You can choose what to eat from a menu just like in a restaurant.

Hospitals have all sorts of special equipment. Doctors and nurses use these tools to help people. Some machines allow doctors to see inside the patient's body.

Doctors may need special classes to learn how to use some machines.

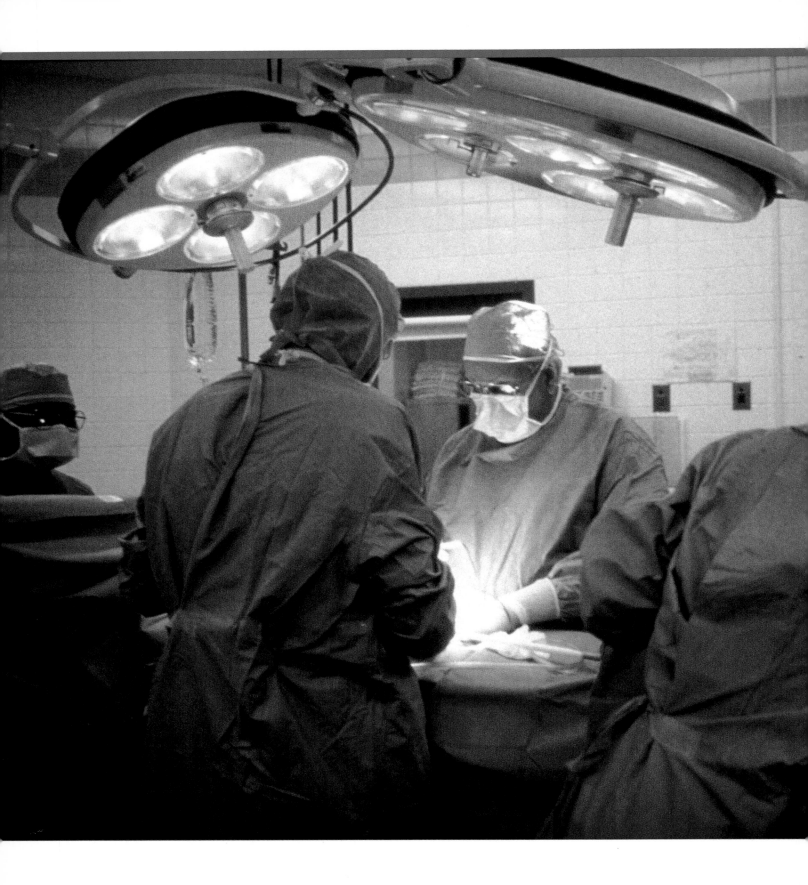

Sometimes doctors need to operate on a patient.
The operating room is very, very clean.
No germs can live here. Everyone wears hats,
gowns, gloves, and masks to keep germs out.

Doctors and nurses scrub before surgery.

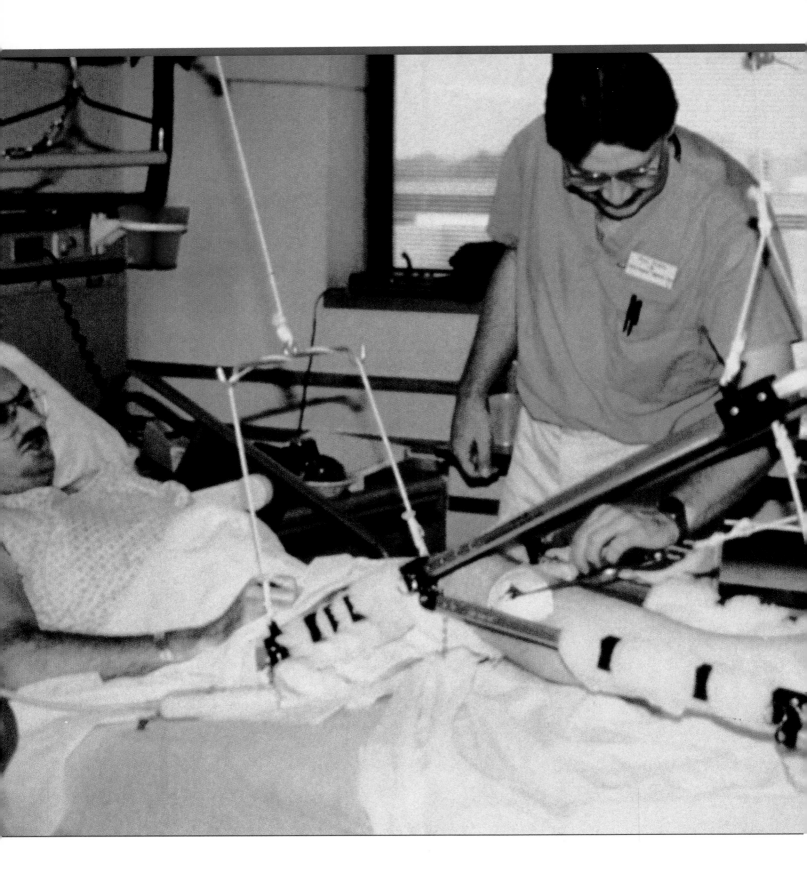

After an operation, a patient rests in a recovery room. Nurses there watch patients very carefully to make sure they are doing well. When the doctor is sure the patient is doing well, the patient is taken back to his or her room.

The nurse is the first person a patient sees when he or she wakes up.

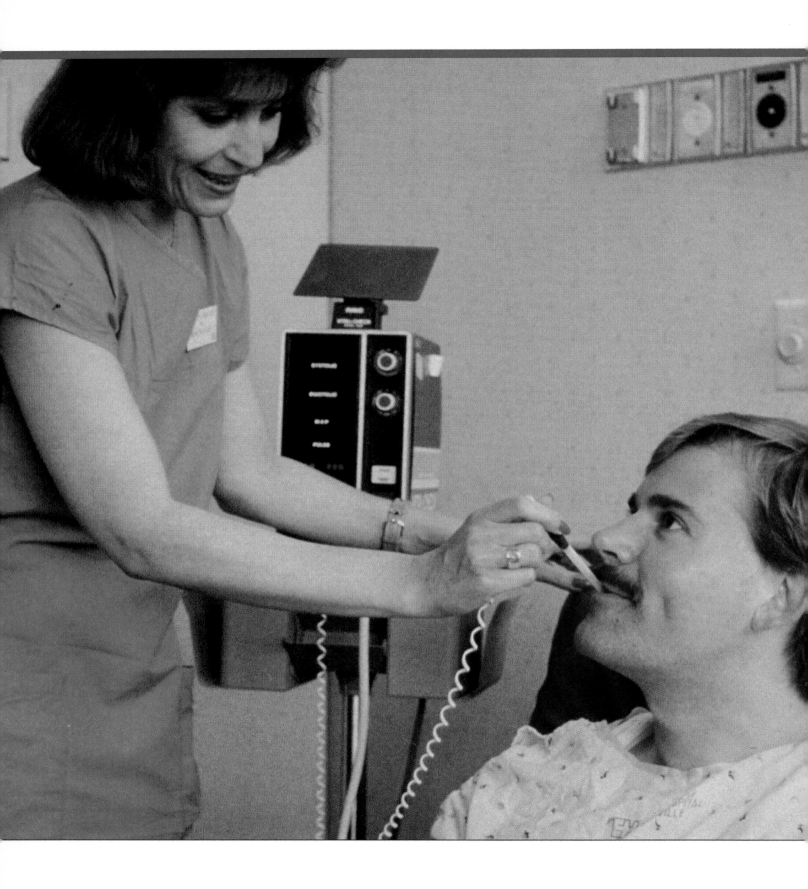

Nurses make sure their patients are comfortable.
They give each one the right medicine.
They keep records of each patient's temperature.
They make sure each one is eating right and
sleeping well.

Nurses check on patients even when they're sleeping.

Patients enjoy having visitors.

Visitors help patients feel better.

They bring the best medicine—a smile.

Once a patient is well, it's time to go home.

Bye, Bye!!!!

GLOSSARY

Admissions—place in the hospital where patients give information about themselves and fill out papers

bone—hard material that makes up the skeleton

cast—material used to cover broken bones that hardens when dry

dietitians—people who are specially trained to plan menus and cook healthy food

Emergency Room—place in the hospital where people who have sudden sickness or injury are taken to receive medical help

germs—things too small to be seen that carry disease

gurneys—high, flat carts on wheels

hospital—place built to help people who are sick or hurt

illness—sickness; not feeling healthy

maternity—motherhood

medicine—substances given to people to help them get better

nurses—people who help people who are sick or need medical attention

operation—the act of cutting into a body to fix something

orderly—name for a person who helps patients

oxygen—air

patient—name for people who are being cared for by a doctor

preemies—premature babies; babies who were born before spending nine months in their mother's body

scrub—clean; wash

surgery—medical treatment by performing an operation

temperature—how hot or cold something is

tonsils—part of the human body found at the back of the throat

x rays—special rays that can go through a covering and see inside an object; for example, in an x-ray photograph the bones of the hand will show up as white objects against a black background.

About the Author

Amy Moses writes books for children, teachers, and parents. She earned her masters degree in education with a Specialty in Reading. Amy is currently writing a novel. She loves reading, writing, making things, and being outdoors.